WILLIAM McKinley

WILLIAM *McKinley*

OUR TWENTY-FIFTH PRESIDENT

By Cynthia A. Klingel and Robert B. Noyed

SPIRIT
of America™

The Child's World®, Inc.
Chanhassen, Minnesota

10

William *McKinley*

Published in the United States of America by The Child's World®, Inc.
PO Box 326 • Chanhassen, MN 55317-0326 • 800-599-READ • www.childsworld.com

Acknowledgments

The Creative Spark: Mary Francis-DeMarois, Project Director; Elizabeth Sirimarco Budd, Series Editor; Robert Court, Design and Art Direction; Janine Graham, Page Layout; Jennifer Moyers, Production

The Child's World®, Inc.: Mary Berendes, Publishing Director; Red Line Editorial, Fact Research; Cindy Klingel, Curriculum Advisor; Robert Noyed, Historical Advisor

Photos

Cover: White House Collection, courtesy White House Historical Association; Courtesy of the Buffalo and Erie County Historical Society: 33, 36; Corbis: 23; Library of Congress Collections: 10, 20, 21, 25-32, 37; Courtesy of the McKinley Museum and National Memorial: 6, 7, 8, 11-16, 18, 22, 24, 34, 35

Registration

The Child's World®, Inc., Spirit of America™, and their associated logos are the sole property and registered trademarks of The Child's World®, Inc.

Library of Congress Cataloging-in-Publication Data

Klingel, Cynthia Fitterer.
   William McKinley : our twenty-fifth president / by Cynthia A. Klingel and Robert B. Noyed.
      p. cm.
   Includes bibliographical references and index.
   ISBN 1-56766-861-5 (lib. bdg. : alk. paper)
   1. McKinley, William, 1843–1901—Juvenile literature. 2. Presidents—United States—
Biography—Juvenile literature. [1. McKinley, William, 1843–1901. 2. Presidents.]
I. Noyed, Robert B. II. Title.
   E711.6 .K59 2001
   973.8'8'092—dc21
                                            00-011459

Contents

Chapter ONE

Early Life

William McKinley, shown here as a young man, was born in Ohio in 1843. He is one of eight U.S. presidents to be elected from that state.

WILLIAM MCKINLEY WAS BORN ON JANUARY 29, 1843, in Niles, Ohio. His father worked very hard to support the family, but they did not have much money. Even though they were poor, William's parents wanted all of their children to be well educated. As a young boy, William attended a one-room schoolhouse in Niles.

In 1852, when William McKinley was nine years old, his family moved to Poland, Ohio. There he attended a private school called the Poland Academy. Living in Poland was a sacrifice for William's father because he had to travel many miles back to his business in Niles. This caused him to be away from home most of the time. For this reason, William became very close to his mother. She was responsible

for raising the children and encouraging them to be successful in school.

William McKinley was a serious student who worked hard at his studies. He enjoyed reading, **debating,** and public speaking. In fact, he was the president of the Poland Academy's first debate club. Like his mother, he was deeply religious. With his religious beliefs and his talent for public speaking, it seemed that William could be an outstanding minister. This made his mother happy. She always hoped that William would become a minister.

In 1860, when he was 17 years old, McKinley entered Allegheny College in

McKinley's parents worked hard to make sure their children were educated and successful. His father was an abolitionist, someone who wanted to end slavery in the United States. His mother taught young William about honesty and faith.

McKinley was born in this unpainted clapboard house in Niles, Ohio. He was the seventh of nine children born to his parents, William and Nancy McKinley.

Pennsylvania. After only a few months, he became very ill and was forced to go home. McKinley planned to return to school as soon as he recovered from his illness. By the time he was well enough to go back, his family could not afford the cost of college. So in 1861, 18-year-old McKinley went to work as a teacher and as a clerk at the post office. He wanted to earn money so he could finish college. Unfortunately, serious events in the United States forced McKinley to delay his return to college even longer.

In the early 1860s, there were many troubles in the United States. For years, people in the North had criticized the Southern states for owning slaves. The Northerners grew more and more certain that there should be an end to slavery and that the slaves should be free. The Southerners grew angrier. Many of them thought they could never run their large farms, called plantations, without the free labor that the slaves provided. They felt that Northerners did not just want them to end slavery, but to change their whole way of life. The arguments between the North and South quickly turned to violence. On April 12, 1861, fighting broke out between the North and the South at Fort Sumter in Charleston, South Carolina. This was the start of the Civil War.

McKinley's cousin, Will, was visiting him when they heard the news of the attack at Fort Sumter. Their loyalty to the **Union** and to the new president of the United States, Abraham Lincoln, was very strong. They decided it was their duty to join the army. Both young men joined in the Ohio Volunteer Infantry.

McKinley became a brave and outstanding soldier. He entered every battle confident

Before the Civil War began, Fort Sumter was running short of supplies. The U.S. government needed to restock it or shut it down. President Lincoln decided the South would consider it a sign of weakness if he closed the fort, so he decided to send supplies and soldiers. Southerners believed this was an act of war.

that he would not be injured. He was sure he would return home to his mother safe and well, just as he had promised her. McKinley's confidence and leadership were recognized by the men in charge, and he was given more responsibility. After especially brave acts, he was made an officer, a leader of other soldiers. He was proud to wear the bars on his uniform that indicated his position of leadership.

10

In 1865, McKinley's service in the army was complete. When he returned home, he was a different man. He had a strong, muscular body and a **disciplined** character. He had also developed a strong interest in politics, the work of the government.

A Man of Strong Character

IN A LETTER TO HIS NEPHEW, JAMES (shown at left), McKinley wrote about the importance of having a strong character. As James was entering the army in the late 1800s, McKinley wrote him that "I am deeply interested in your success and I want you to be a good soldier. Do everything the best you know how." Along with the advice about being a good soldier, McKinley offered James advice about his behavior. "Be careful about your writing. See that your words are spelled correctly. Better have a little pocket dictionary with you. It mars an official paper or letter to have a word misspelled." He also encouraged James to have a strong moral character. "Look after your diet and living. Keep your life and your speech both clean, and be brave."

Chapter TWO

Political Leader

McKinley's Civil War experience had a great impact on him as he thought about what he wanted to do with his life.

AFTER HIS SERVICE IN THE CIVIL WAR, McKinley became interested in the world of politics and the possibility of becoming a lawyer. When he returned to Ohio in 1865, he began studying law with Judge Charles Glidden. About one year later, McKinley entered law school in Albany, New York. After completing his studies, he passed his law exam, became a lawyer, and settled in Canton, Ohio. He worked with a local judge for a short time, then McKinley opened his own law office. He won his first case as a lawyer and earned $25 for the work. At that time, $25 was a large amount of money.

McKinley quickly became an important part of the community. His deep faith and simple lifestyle were a perfect match for the

young town of Canton. People were drawn to his thoughtfulness, his friendly laugh, and his pleasing personality. He was able to make friends with people in many different groups in the community. He became the head of the Sunday school in the First Methodist Church and president of the YMCA. After only one year in Canton, McKinley had become popular and was known as an easy-going, faithful neighbor, an open-minded community leader, an able lawyer, and an excellent public speaker. In 1869, this popularity helped him get elected to his first public office, prosecuting attorney of Stark County.

McKinley worked as a lawyer at this office in Canton, Ohio. He became known in town as an honest, hardworking man. He made friends easily and was soon elected to his first political office, the job of prosecuting attorney.

McKinley was a handsome, friendly man who was popular with the people of his hometown. His personality helped him win his first political office —and many others.

A prosecuting attorney is a lawyer who works with the police to make sure that people who break the law go to jail.

Another important event happened to McKinley in 1869. While doing business at the bank, McKinley met Ida Saxton, the daughter of the local banker. Ida was a beautiful, well-educated young woman. McKinley and Ida fell in love and were married in January of 1871. Ida gave birth to the couple's first daughter, Katherine, on Christmas Day in 1871. Their second daughter, Ida, was born in 1873. But young Ida was unhealthy and died before she was five months old. That same year, Ida's mother also died. Two years later, Katherine died from a serious illness. This was a very difficult time for Mrs. McKinley. After the death of her mother and two daughters, she became ill with depression and epilepsy. This disease caused her to

▶ One story says that
William McKinley
and Ida Saxton had
been walking together
one day when it came
time to part. William
said, "I don't like
these partings. I think
we ought not to
part after this." Ida
agreed, and the couple
decided to marry on
January 25, 1871.

*Ida Saxton was a lovely, well-educated young woman from Canton
who was the daughter of a successful banker. Many of the young men
in town were interested in her. But once she met William McKinley,
she made up her mind to marry him. She would have no other suitor.*

The McKinley's first daughter, Katherine, died when she was only four years old. This was just one of many family tragedies the couple faced in a short period of time. Mrs. McKinley became weak and ill after that. She was very dependent on her husband, who cared for her for the rest of his life.

have attacks that sometimes made her faint. Ida lived the rest of her life struggling with these illnesses. Thankfully, her husband was devoted to taking care of her.

During this difficult family time, McKinley continued to be successful in his work. He became increasingly interested in politics, the work of the government. He decided to run for the House of Representatives, part of the U.S. Congress. With this decision, McKinley left his law practice. He was elected to the House, moved with Ida to Washington, D.C., and began a long and respected career in government. One of his most important accomplishments was the McKinley Tariff of 1890, which helped protect American companies from foreign competition. This tariff was a tax on foreign goods that made **imported** products more expensive. It encouraged Americans to buy items made in the United States because they cost less than foreign goods. McKinley believed this would help not only the wealthy businessmen who owned American companies, but also the workers who made the goods. The tariff made McKinley popular with Americans both rich and poor.

McKinley served seven terms in the U.S. House of Representatives. In Washington, he was known as a polite and patient man. Other politicians remarked that he was the only man in Congress who had no enemies. Even so, he was defeated for reelection in 1891. He and Ida returned to Canton.

Later that year, McKinley made a political comeback. He was elected governor of Ohio and served from 1892 until 1895. As governor, McKinley proposed laws to protect railroad workers. He tried to find ways to stop child labor. At that time, it was not uncommon for children to work long hours at difficult jobs. He also supported laws to deal with problems between workers and large businesses. During his time as governor, McKinley met a man named Mark Hanna, a powerful businessman who owned several mines. Hanna helped to

Interesting Facts

▸ When McKinley ran for the U.S. House of Representatives in 1876, he began wearing a scarlet carnation on the collar of his coat. He almost always wore a red flower. In 1904, the state of Ohio adopted the scarlet carnation as its official state flower in his honor.

McKinley was a successful lawyer before he was elected to the House of Representatives. Working as a congressman came at a price, however, for he earned only half of what he had as a lawyer. "Before I went to Congress I had $10,000 and a practice worth $10,000," said McKinley. "Now I haven't either."

raise money for McKinley's political **campaigns.** In fact, he helped to raise more than $3.5 million for McKinley's first presidential campaign. This was a record amount of money at that time. Hanna also became one of McKinley's most important **advisers.**

In 1896, the **Republican Party** chose McKinley as their **candidate** for the upcoming presidential election. The vice presidential candidate was Garret Hobart, and Mark Hanna managed the campaign. At this time in history, presidential candidates did most of their campaigning by riding trains across the United States. They stopped in towns and cities along the way to give speeches and meet the people. McKinley's opponent, William Jennings Bryan, was a wonderful speaker. He used this strategy for his campaign. People everywhere were able to meet Bryan and hear him speak.

Because McKinley's wife needed his care, he would not leave her to campaign in this way. Instead, he held a "front-porch" campaign from his home. More than 750,000 people traveled to Canton to hear him give campaign speeches. Newspapers all across the United States printed his words. In addition, McKinley was the first

This 1896 campaign poster shows McKinley and the vice presidential candidate, Garret Hobart.

PROTECTION AND SOUND MONEY

Interesting Facts

▶ McKinley and his wife loved flowers. After he was elected president, the rooms of the White House were always decorated with fresh flowers.

candidate to hand out campaign buttons and other items to promote himself as a candidate. He was very successful in the campaign for the presidency. In fact, he won the largest number of the people's votes since Ulysses S. Grant in 1872. With the support of the people, McKinley was elected the 25th president of the United States in 1896.

WHAT DOES A PRESIDENT DO DURING EACH DAY? McKINLEY HAD A BUSY AND interesting schedule. He usually would have his breakfast at about nine o'clock each morning, read the newspaper, and be at his desk by 10 o'clock. He would then have meetings with other officials until he left at about 1:30 in the afternoon for lunch with his wife. He returned to his desk by about 2:30 and worked until 4:30.

Almost every day, he would take a carriage drive with Mrs. McKinley through the streets of Washington, D.C. Some days he would ride several miles on horseback or take walks near the White House. He would then return to his office to read telegrams from the day and to look at the evening newspaper. President McKinley would have dinner at about 7 PM and always appeared at the dinner table nicely dressed. After attending social activities, McKinley would return to his office and work until about midnight each night. McKinley attended church every Sunday and never worked or attended public events on Sundays.

21

Chapter THREE

A World Power

As president, McKinley hoped to focus on problems at home. Unfortunately, crises with other countries took up most of his time.

IN HIS 1896 CAMPAIGN FOR PRESIDENT, MCKINLEY talked a lot about **domestic** issues that affected the people of the United States. He remained committed to these issues, but the years of his presidency involved **foreign policy** issues and provided opportunities for the United States to become a world power.

During his first two years as president, the United States became involved in the **conflict** between Cuba and Spain. Cuba was fighting for its independence from Spain. Many politicians wanted the United States to help Cuba. Even many newspapers became involved in the issue and encouraged the president to take action. McKinley felt pressured by public opinion.

In January of 1898, he sent the battleship U.S.S. *Maine* to Havana, Cuba, to protect

American interests there. McKinley also tried to get Spain to **negotiate** with Cuba on the issue of independence. Unfortunately, a tragedy occurred that forced McKinley to make a difficult decision. On February 15, 1898, the U.S.S. *Maine* mysteriously exploded while in the Havana harbor. More than 260 of the ship's 354 crew members were killed in the explosion. There was no way, however, to prove that Spain was involved in this incident. But many

At first, McKinley did not want to get involved in the problems between Cuba and Spain. But after the explosion of the U.S.S. Maine, it seemed that the United States could not avoid going to war.

23

Interesting Facts

▶ The sinking of the U.S.S. *Maine* caused many Americans to call for an attack on Spain. The phrase "Remember the *Maine*" was used by people who wanted the United States to attack Spain.

Americans believed Spain was behind the explosion, and wanted the United States to declare war.

McKinley knew that a war with Spain was likely, but he attempted to resolve the conflict in other ways. He sent messages to Spain demanding an end to the conflict in Cuba. He also demanded that Cuba be given its independence. McKinley was opposed to war. He searched for ways to peacefully end the conflict. He said, "War should never be entered upon until every agency of peace has failed." He said peace was always preferable to war.

Once the United States declared war on Spain, McKinley was dedicated to victory. He is shown here (seated at center) meeting with a general and his staff.

Unfortunately, his attempts to negotiate a peaceful solution failed. On April 25, 1898, the U.S. Congress declared war on Spain.

The Spanish-American War involved battles on the island of Cuba and on the seas surrounding it. Because Spain also had colonies in the Philippines and other islands in the Pacific Ocean, the United States sent ships and troops to those areas as well. The war lasted only about 100 days before the United States won. The most important battle took place in Cuba. The Battle of San Juan Hill was led by Theodore "Teddy" Roosevelt and a group of soldiers called the Rough Riders. During the battle, U.S. ships formed a **blockade** in the Santiago Harbor and trapped the Spanish fleet of ships. Roosevelt then led his Rough Riders up San Juan Hill and took possession of the area. The Spanish-American War ended shortly after this battle.

In August of 1898, the United States and Spain signed an **armistice** to end the war. This agreement became known as the Treaty of Paris. After it was signed, the United States took control of Cuba, Puerto Rico, and Guam. For $20 million, it took over the Philippines

Future president Teddy Roosevelt led a group of soldiers known as the Rough Riders. They fought the Battle of San Juan Hill, which helped end the Spanish-American War.

9003—Company of Boxers, Tien-Tsin, China.

A group of Boxers is shown in the print above. The Boxers rebelled against foreigners trying to have a too-powerful presence in their country (China). This is an old-fashioned type of print called a stereograph. These prints could be placed in a machine that made the images appear three dimensional.

as well. By taking over these areas, the United States became one of the most powerful nations in the world.

After the Spanish-American War, McKinley took several steps to demonstrate the United States' position as a world power. Now that it had control of the Philippines and Guam, the United States became more interested in the politics of Asian countries. In 1898, McKinley issued what was called the "Open Door" trade **policy** with China. This policy allowed the United States the opportunity to buy Chinese goods, as well as to sell American goods in China.

The Open Door Policy was announced in early 1900. A group of Chinese people known as the Boxers were angry about it. They wanted to push all foreign countries out of their nation. To show that the United States supported the Open Door Policy, McKinley sent 5,000 U.S. soldiers to China to help Germany, Japan, Russia, and other countries end the war that was known as the Boxer **Rebellion.** These countries were successful in stopping the rebellion, and the Open Door Policy with China remained in effect until the 1920s.

The United States was not the only country that tried to crush the Boxer Rebellion. Many nations came together to fight. Here Japanese soldiers are shown in battle against the Boxers.

28

THE ROUGH RIDERS WERE A GROUP OF AMERICAN SOLDIERS IN THE Spanish-American War who were led by Theodore "Teddy" Roosevelt. Before the start of the war, Roosevelt was an assistant secretary of the navy. He quit his job and formed a group of fighting men that became known as the Rough Riders. The group was officially called the First United States Volunteer Cavalry. A cavalry is part of an army that fights on horseback. Roosevelt's troop became known as the Rough Riders because it was made up of many cowboys, hunters, and outdoorsmen from the western United States. There were also large numbers of Native Americans and African Americans who joined the troop. A year before the Spanish-American War, Roosevelt spoke out about the need for the United States to help Cuba. When it became clear that the United States would be involved in a war, army surgeon Leonard Wood and Roosevelt were asked to form this cavalry group. The Rough Riders trained for only one month before they were sent into battle. In 1899, Roosevelt published a book called *Rough Riders* that included his personal story about his adventures with this famous group of soldiers.

Chapter FOUR

The Final Years

McKinley was a popular president. In fact, both Republicans and Democrats voted for him.

PRESIDENT MCKINLEY GUIDED THE COUNTRY through the Spanish-American War and led it to a position as a world power. This made him popular among the American people. As the 1900 presidential election approached, McKinley was again selected as the Republican **nominee** for president. The only question about McKinley's campaign was who would be the candidate for vice president. Garret Hobart, who served as McKinley's vice president during his first term, had died in 1899. McKinley needed to find a new running mate. He and the Republicans chose Theodore Roosevelt, who was then the governor of New York.

As in 1896, McKinley's opponent in the election was William Jennings Bryan. During the campaign, Bryan attacked McKinley on

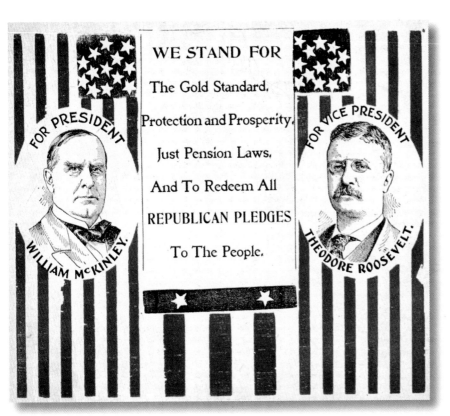

WE STAND FOR

The Gold Standard,

Protection and Prosperity,

Just Pension Laws,

And To Redeem All

REPUBLICAN PLEDGES

To The People.

FOR PRESIDENT

WILLIAM McKINLEY.

FOR VICE PRESIDENT

THEODORE ROOSEVELT.

This campaign poster shows McKinley and the new vice presidential candidate, Theodore Roosevelt.

the issues of American **imperialism,** which means that he thought the government had too much control over other countries. Bryan was against U.S. control of the Philippines, Puerto Rico, and other countries. He also said that McKinley had allowed large businesses to grow too powerful.

Even though McKinley did not campaign during the election, he easily defeated Bryan and began his second term as president of the United States in March of 1901. McKinley planned to spend more time dealing with domestic problems instead of foreign issues.

In 1900, William Jennings Bryan ran against McKinley for the second time. Bryan believed the United States should not have so much power in other countries. The cartoon above shows McKinley raising the American flag and helping the United States expand its power in other countries, while Bryan tries to chop it down. The cartoon at right shows Bryan blowing up a balloon, symbolizing McKinley's imperialism.

He had hoped to address the problems of child labor, the poor treatment of workers, and the abuse of African Americans. But McKinley never had a chance to make a difference in these areas.

In 1901, there was a major event held in Buffalo, New York, called the Pan-American Exposition. The Exposition was celebrating 100 years of progress in North and South America. On September 5, McKinley gave a speech at the Exposition. It was an important speech about America's role in the world. It was well received by both Americans and people from other countries.

The next day, September 6, McKinley appeared at the Exposition again. This time, he was greeting visitors at a public reception. One man, Leon Czolgosz, waited in line to shake hands with the president. Instead of shaking McKinley's hand, Czolgosz shot him twice. One bullet bounced off a button on McKinley's chest, but the other bullet went through his stomach, colon, and kidney, stopping in the muscles of his back. McKinley was rushed to the emergency medical hospital at the Exposition. Surgeons operated immediately, but they could not find the bullet. In fact, they did not realize at the time that the bullet had damaged any organs other than the stomach. They repaired the stomach and were hopeful for a full recovery.

The McKinleys arrived at the Pan-American Exposition in a horse-drawn carriage. The president was looking forward to meeting with people at this great event.

▶ One tribute after McKinley's death was a farewell from Native American leaders. Chiefs Geronimo, Blue Horse, Flat Iron, and Red Shirt joined 700 Native Americans from the Indian Congress at the Exposition to say goodbye to the man they had considered their great friend.

McKinley seemed to be recovering in the days after the shooting. Everyone was confident that the president would soon be back to work. On September 14, eight days after the shooting, the president died from infection caused by the bullet. Theodore Roosevelt became the 26th president.

The nation was in shock. Citizens of foreign countries were stunned because the

After her husband's death, Ida McKinley (right) was devastated. "He is gone," she said to friends, "and life is dark to me now."

world had lost a great leader. People forgot their political differences as they mourned the loss of President McKinley.

Ida McKinley was devastated by her husband's death. She was very sad and greatly missed him. It is believed that she visited McKinley's grave almost every day. Ida lived with her younger sister until her death in 1907.

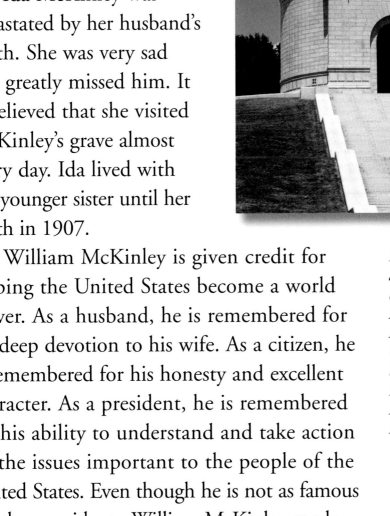

In 1911, Congress created an association charged with building the National McKinley Birthplace Memorial, located in Niles, Ohio. The memorial is a building made of marble. Inside are the McKinley Museum and the McKinley Memorial Library.

William McKinley is given credit for helping the United States become a world power. As a husband, he is remembered for his deep devotion to his wife. As a citizen, he is remembered for his honesty and excellent character. As a president, he is remembered for his ability to understand and take action on the issues important to the people of the United States. Even though he is not as famous as other presidents, William McKinley made the United States into one of the world's most powerful nations.

"I DID MY DUTY." THOSE WERE THE WORDS OF LEON CZOLGOSZ AFTER HE shot President McKinley. Czolgosz, shown in the police photograph below, was a 28-year-old man who lived in Cleveland, Ohio. He traveled to the Pan-American Exposition in Buffalo, New York, three days before he shot the president. In his confession to the police, he described his plans to shoot McKinley. He told police how he hid his gun with a handkerchief and described how he shot the president. Police said that Czolgosz seemed proud of what he had done. He did not have many friends and spent much of his free time reading newspapers and books. Over time, Czolgosz

came to hate the American system of government. He believed that all government officials were against working people. He thought that the president was "an enemy of the people" and that it was acceptable to kill him. Czolgosz shot McKinley on September 6, 1901. President McKinley died from the wounds on September 14.

1843 William McKinley is born on January 29 in Niles, Ohio. He is the seventh of nine children. His parents are William and Nancy.

1852 McKinley's family moves to Poland, Ohio, so the children have more opportunities for a quality education. McKinley becomes a leading student at the Poland Academy, excelling in speaking and debate activities.

1860 McKinley enters Allegheny College in Meadville, Pennsylvania, but falls ill and must return home before the end of the school year.

1861 McKinley teaches and works in the post office to earn money to return to college. In April, the Civil War breaks out at Fort Sumter, South Carolina. McKinley and his cousin Will join the Union army to fight in the Civil War as part of the Ohio Volunteer Infantry.

1865 McKinley completes honorable service in the army and returns home to Ohio. He begins to study law, first with Judge Charles Glidden and then at the Albany Law School.

1867 McKinley settles in Canton, Ohio, and begins practicing law.

1869 McKinley is elected to his first public office, that of prosecuting attorney of Stark County, Ohio. He meets Miss Ida Saxton, the beautiful daughter of a wealthy Canton banker.

1871 McKinley and Ida marry in January. A daughter, Katherine, is born to the McKinleys on Christmas Day.

1873 A second daughter, Ida, is born to the McKinleys but only lives four and a half months.

1875 Katherine dies at the age of four.

1876 McKinley is elected to the U.S. House of Representatives. He is reelected for six more terms and serves until 1891.

1890 McKinley proposes the McKinley Tariff, which protects American businesses from foreign competition.

1891 McKinley is elected governor of Ohio. He serves in this position for the next four years. As governor, he proposes laws to help railroad workers and deals with the problem of child labor. He helps solve problems between workers and business owners. While governor, he meets Mark Hanna, who will be an important supporter in his future campaign for the presidency.

1896 The Republican Party selects McKinley as its presidential candidate. Mark Hanna raises more than $3.5 million for the campaign. McKinley is elected president of the United States. Garret Hobart is his vice president.

1898 The battleship U.S.S. *Maine* mysteriously explodes in Havana, Cuba. More than 260 crew members are killed in the explosion. Americans blame Spain for the attack and encourage McKinley to declare war. The United States declares war on Spain. The Spanish-American War begins on April 25 and ends about 100 days later. Theodore "Teddy" Roosevelt and the Rough Riders win the most important battle of the war, the Battle of San Juan Hill. After the war, the United States takes control of Cuba, Puerto Rico, Guam, and the Philippines. McKinley begins the Open Door Policy in trade relations with China.

1899 Vice President Garret Hobart dies.

1900 Some Chinese people, upset with foreign involvement in their government, start the Boxer Rebellion. McKinley is reelected president of the United States. Theodore Roosevelt is the vice president.

1901 In his second term, McKinley plans to spend more time dealing with domestic issues. Unfortunately, he has little time in office. He is shot twice by Leon Czolgosz at the Pan-American Exposition in Buffalo, New York, on September 6. Surgeons cannot find the bullet, and a serious infection sets in. He dies from complications of the gunshot wound on September 14. Vice President Theodore Roosevelt becomes the 26th president.

1907 Ida Saxton McKinley dies.

1911 Congress creates the National McKinley Birthplace Memorial Association, which builds a memorial to the president in Niles, Ohio.

Glossary TERMS

advisers (ad-VY-zerz)
Advisers are people who give advice or information to others. When he was president, McKinley had advisers who helped him make decisions.

armistice (AR-meh-stis)
An armistice is an agreement to stop fighting. The Treaty of Paris was an armistice that ended fighting during the Spanish-American War.

blockade (blaw-KAYD)
A blockade keeps people and supplies from moving in or out of an area. U.S. ships formed a blockade in Cuba to trap Spanish ships during the Battle of San Juan Hill.

campaigns (kam-PAYNZ)
Campaigns are the activities involved in running for an election. A campaign often includes giving speeches and attending rallies.

candidate (KAN-dih-det)
A candidate is a person running in an election. The Republicans chose McKinley as their candidate for president in both 1896 and 1900.

conflict (KON-flikt)
A conflict is a disagreement. The Spanish-American War started with a conflict between Spain and Cuba.

debating (dih-BAY-ting)
Debating is taking part in a contest in which opponents argue on opposite sides of an issue. While at the Poland Academy, McKinley was active in debating clubs.

disciplined (DIS-eh-plind)
If a person is disciplined, he or she has good self-control, is orderly, and follows rules. McKinley was disciplined.

domestic (deh-MES-tik)
Domestic means having to do with one's own country instead of a foreign country. McKinley planned to pay more attention to domestic problems during his second term.

**foreign policy
(FOR-un PAWL-uh-see)**
Foreign policy concerns how a country should deal with other countries. McKinley was very involved in U.S. foreign policy.

imperialism (im-PEER-ee-ul-iz-im)
If a nation supports imperialism, it wants to rule or have authority over other countries. William Jennings Bryan was against imperialism.

imported (im-POR-ted)
If goods are imported, they are brought in from another country to be sold. The McKinley Tariff placed a tax on imported goods.

negotiate (ne-GOH-she-ayt)
If people negotiate, they talk things over and try to come to an agreement. McKinley tried to get Spain to negotiate with Cuba.

nominee (nom-ih-NEE)
A nominee is a person whom others choose to run for a political office. McKinley was the Republican Party's nominee for president in 1896 and 1900.

policy (PAWL-uh-see)
A policy is a plan made to help run a government or other organization. The Boxers of China were against McKinley's Open Door Policy.

rebellion (rih-BEL-yen)
A rebellion is a fight against one's government. A group of Chinese people started the Boxer Rebellion to push foreign countries out of China.

Republican Party (ree-PUB-lih-ken PAR-tee)
The Republican Party is one of the two major U.S. political parties. Political parties are groups of people who share similar ideas about how to run a government. McKinley belonged to the Republican Party.

union (YOON-yen)
A union is the joining together of two people or groups of people, such as states. The Union is another name for the United States.

Our PRESIDENTS

President	Birthplace	Life Span	Presidency	Political Party	First Lady
George Washington	Virginia	1732–1799	1789–1797	None	Martha Dandridge Custis Washington
John Adams	Massachusetts	1735–1826	1797–1801	Federalist	Abigail Smith Adams
Thomas Jefferson	Virginia	1743–1826	1801–1809	Democratic-Republican	widower
James Madison	Virginia	1751–1836	1809–1817	Democratic Republican	Dolley Payne Todd Madison
James Monroe	Virginia	1758–1831	1817–1825	Democratic Republican	Elizabeth Kortright Monroe
John Quincy Adams	Massachusetts	1767–1848	1825–1829	Democratic-Republican	Louisa Johnson Adams
Andrew Jackson	South Carolina	1767–1845	1829–1837	Democrat	widower
Martin Van Buren	New York	1782–1862	1837–1841	Democrat	widower
William H. Harrison	Virginia	1773–1841	1841	Whig	Anna Symmes Harrison
John Tyler	Virginia	1790–1862	1841–1845	Whig	Letitia Christian Tyler / Julia Gardiner Tyler
James K. Polk	North Carolina	1795–1849	1845–1849	Democrat	Sarah Childress Polk

42

President	Birthplace	Life Span	Presidency	Political Party	First Lady
Zachary Taylor	Virginia	1784–1850	1849–1850	Whig	Margaret Mackall Smith Taylor
Millard Fillmore	New York	1800–1874	1850–1853	Whig	Abigail Powers Fillmore
Franklin Pierce	New Hampshire	1804–1869	1853–1857	Democrat	Jane Means Appleton Pierce
James Buchanan	Pennsylvania	1791–1868	1857–1861	Democrat	never married
Abraham Lincoln	Kentucky	1809–1865	1861–1865	Republican	Mary Todd Lincoln
Andrew Johnson	North Carolina	1808–1875	1865–1869	Democrat	Eliza McCardle Johnson
Ulysses S. Grant	Ohio	1822–1885	1869–1877	Republican	Julia Dent Grant
Rutherford B. Hayes	Ohio	1822–1893	1877–1881	Republican	Lucy Webb Hayes
James A. Garfield	Ohio	1831–1881	1881	Republican	Lucretia Rudolph Garfield
Chester A. Arthur	Vermont	1829–1886	1881–1885	Republican	widower
Grover Cleveland	New Jersey	1837–1908	1885–1889	Democrat	Frances Folsom Cleveland

Our PRESIDENTS

President	Birthplace	Life Span	Presidency	Political Party	First Lady
Benjamin Harrison	Ohio	1833–1901	1889–1893	Republican	Caroline Scott Harrison
Grover Cleveland	New Jersey	1837–1908	1893–1897	Democrat	Frances Folsom Cleveland
William McKinley	Ohio	1843–1901	1897–1901	Republican	Ida Saxton McKinley
Theodore Roosevelt	New York	1858–1919	1901–1909	Republican	Edith Kermit Carow Roosevelt
William H. Taft	Ohio	1857–1930	1909–1913	Republican	Helen Herron Taft
Woodrow Wilson	Virginia	1856–1924	1913–1921	Democrat	Ellen L. Axson Wilson Edith Bolling Galt Wilson
Warren G. Harding	Ohio	1865–1923	1921–1923	Republican	Florence Kling De Wolfe Harding
Calvin Coolidge	Vermont	1872–1933	1923–1929	Republican	Grace Goodhue Coolidge
Herbert C. Hoover	Iowa	1874–1964	1929–1933	Republican	Lou Henry Hoover
Franklin D. Roosevelt	New York	1882–1945	1933–1945	Democrat	Anna Eleanor Roosevelt Roosevelt
Harry S. Truman	Missouri	1884–1972	1945–1953	Democrat	Elizabeth Wallace Truman

Our PRESIDENTS

President	Birthplace	Life Span	Presidency	Political Party	First Lady
Dwight D. Eisenhower	Texas	1890–1969	1953–1961	Republican	Mary "Mamie" Doud Eisenhower
John F. Kennedy	Massachusetts	1917–1963	1961–1963	Democrat	Jacqueline Bouvier Kennedy
Lyndon B. Johnson	Texas	1908–1973	1963–1969	Democrat	Claudia Alta Taylor Johnson
Richard M. Nixon	California	1913–1994	1969–1974	Republican	Thelma Catherine Ryan Nixon
Gerald Ford	Nebraska	1913–	1974–1977	Republican	Elizabeth "Betty" Bloomer Warren Ford
James Carter	Georgia	1924–	1977–1981	Democrat	Rosalynn Smith Carter
Ronald Reagan	Illinois	1911–	1981–1989	Republican	Nancy Davis Reagan
George Bush	Massachusetts	1924–	1989–1993	Republican	Barbara Pierce Bush
William Clinton	Arkansas	1946–	1993–2001	Democrat	Hillary Rodham Clinton
George W. Bush	Connecticut	1946–	2001–	Republican	Laura Welch Bush

45

Presidential FACTS

Qualifications
To run for president, a candidate must
- be at least 35 years old
- be a citizen who was born in the United States
- have lived in the United States for 14 years

Term of Office
A president's term of office is four years. No president can stay in office for more than two terms.

Election Date
The presidential election takes place every four years on the first Tuesday of November.

Inauguration Date
Presidents are inaugurated on January 20.

Oath of Office
I do solemnly swear I will faithfully execute the office of the President of the United States and will to the best of my ability preserve, protect, and defend the Constitution of the United States.

Write a Letter to the President
One of the best things about being a U.S. citizen is that Americans get to participate in their government. They can speak out if they feel government leaders aren't doing their jobs. They can also praise leaders who are going the extra mile. Do you have something you'd like the president to do? Should the president worry more about the environment and encourage people to recycle? Should the government spend more money on our schools? You can write a letter to the president to say how you feel!

1600 Pennsylvania Avenue
Washington, D.C. 20500

You can even send an e-mail to: president@whitehouse.gov

For Further INFORMATION

Internet Sites

Learn more about William McKinley:
http://www.ipl.org/ref/POTUS/wmmckinley.html
http://www.mckinley.lib.oh.us/museum/biography.htm

Visit Mount McKinley and Denali National Park:
http://www.denalinationalpark.com/McKinley.htm

Find out more about Teddy Roosevelt and the Rough Riders:
http://www.bartleby.com/51/

Visit the McKinley Memorial Library:
http://www.mckinley.lib.oh.us/library/default.htm

View items in the McKinley Museum:
http://www.mckinley.lib.oh.us/museum/inside/museumpic.htm

Learn more about the Spanish-American War:
http://spanam.simplenet.com/basics.htm

Learn more about all the presidents and visit the White House:
http://www.whitehouse.gov/WH/glimps/presidents/html/presidents/html
http://www.thepresidency.org/presinfo.htm
http://www.american presidents.org/

Books

Collins, Mary. *The Spanish-American War* (Cornerstones of Freedom). Chicago: Childrens Press, 1998.

Gaines, Ann Graham. *Teddy Roosevelt: Our Twenty-Sixth President.* Chanhassen, MN: The Child's World, 2002.

Kent, Zachary. *William McKinley.* Chicago: Childrens Press, 1988.

Index